To

_____

From

_____

Date

_____

Daily Inspirations of Joy

© 2008 Christian Art Gifts, RSA
          Christian Art Gifts Inc., IL, USA

First edition 2008
Second edition 2014

Designed by Christian Art Gifts

Scripture quotations are taken from the *Holy Bible*, New International
Version® NIV®. Copyright © 1973, 1978, 1984 by International Bible
Society. Used by permission of Zondervan Publishing House. All
rights reserved.

Scripture quotations marked NLT are taken from the *Holy Bible*,
New Living Translation®, first edition, copyright © 1996. Used by
permission of Tyndale House Publishers, Inc., Carol Stream, Illinois
60188. All rights reserved.

Printed in China

ISBN 978-1-4321-1021-5

© All rights reserved. No part of this book may be reproduced in any
form without permission in writing from the publisher, except in the
case of brief quotations embodied in critical articles or reviews.

14 15 16 17 18 19 20 21 22 23 – 12 11 10 9 8 7 6 5 4 3

Daily Inspirations of

Joy

Carolyn Larsen

christian
art gifts®

Introduction

❧

Would you describe your life as joyous? Do those closest to you consider you to be a joy-filled person?

It's true that joy and happiness are not the same. Happiness is based on circumstances and therefore ebbs and flows; joy comes from the heart and is therefore not dependent on what's happening in your life.

Joy comes from a deep trust in God. Believing that He is in control of all things and yielding your life to Him brings joy.

Joy Because Jesus Came

Life certainly has its ups and downs; its joys and sorrows. We struggle through the sorrows and celebrate the joys. It's fun to celebrate the joys of life and because of this, most of us celebrate for all we're worth. Here's an interesting idea though: the greatest joy life has to offer, the one thing you celebrate the most, is enhanced and expanded when you understand that Jesus came to earth because He loves you.

God showed just how much He loves mankind when He sent His only Son. Jesus coming to earth as a baby was the beginning of God's plan to give mankind a chance to reconnect with Him.

Because Jesus came, lived, died and rose again, your sins can be forgiven and you can have the hope of heaven and being with God for eternity. Now, that's a reason for joy that makes everything else shine brighter!

"For God so loved the world that He gave His one and only Son, that whoever believes in Him shall not perish but have eternal life."

John 3:16

God demonstrates His own love for us in this: While we were still sinners, Christ died for us.

Romans 5:8

This is how we know what love is: Jesus Christ laid down His life for us. And we ought to lay down our lives for our brothers.

1 John 3:16

This is love: not that we loved God, but that He loved us and sent His Son as an atoning sacrifice for our sins.

1 John 4:10

Because of His great love for us, God, who is rich in mercy, made us alive with Christ even when we were dead in transgressions.

Ephesians 2:4-5

This is how God showed His love among us: He sent His one and only Son into the world that we might live through Him.

I John 4:9

For to us a child is born, to us a son is given, and the government will be on His shoulders. And He will be called Wonderful Counselor, Mighty God, Everlasting Father, Prince of Peace.

Isaiah 9:6

Surely goodness and love will follow me all the days of my life, and I will dwell in the house of the Lord forever.

Psalm 23:6

No man ever loved like Jesus.
He taught the blind to see and the
dumb to speak. He died on the cross to
save us. He bore our sins.
And now God says, "Because He did,
I can forgive you."

~ Billy Graham

❧

Dear Father, I can't begin to imagine how it felt for You to decide to sacrifice Your own Son ... for me. That is the greatest expression of love I can imagine. Thank You so much that Jesus came, lived, taught, died and rose again ... for me.

Amen.

Joy Because of Jesus' Example

Life is a learning experience, isn't it? Each phase of life brings new circumstances and situations that you have to adjust to and handle with grace. Just when you think things are running smoothly ... everything changes again. It's not easy to handle these changes with grace. Do you sometimes want the world to stop so you can get off for a while? Of course you don't *really* want that, but a little peace would be nice.

Talking about handling changes with grace makes one think about Jesus. One minute He had crowds of people cheering for Him; throwing their coats on the ground before Him and waving palm branches. A short time later those same people were shouting, "Crucify Him!" Whew! That's a change in attitude. But, as always, Jesus faced even that change with grace and obedience. We can rejoice in the example of how Jesus lived to show us how to handle the changes in our own lives: Ask for help when you need it, be gracious and be obedient. Joy will follow.

The law was given through Moses; grace and truth came through Jesus Christ.

John 1:17

Your attitude should be the same as that of Christ Jesus ... taking the very nature of a servant, being made in human likeness.

Philippians 2:5, 7

"Take My yoke upon you and learn from Me, for I am gentle and humble in heart, and you will find rest for your souls."

Matthew 11:29

Although He was a son, He learned obedience from what He suffered and, once made perfect, He became the source of eternal salvation for all who obey Him.

Hebrews 5:8-9

We love because He first loved us.

1 John 4:19

Be imitators of God, therefore, as dearly loved children and live a life of love, just as Christ loved us and gave Himself up for us as a fragrant offering and sacrifice to God.

Ephesians 5:1-2

"*Abba*, Father," He said, "everything is possible for You. Take this cup from Me. Yet not what I will, but what You will."

Mark 14:36

Being found in appearance as a man, He humbled Himself and became obedient to death – even death on a cross!

Philippians 2:8

Jesus Christ turns life right-side-up,
and heaven outside-in.

~ Carl F. H. Henry

❧

Dear Father, because Jesus lived and breathed on this earth, I know that He understands what life is like here. He knows the temptations, the struggles, the dailyness of life. I'm so grateful that by reading and learning how He made it through and how He related to people and to You, I can learn how to do that too.

Amen.

Joy in Friendships

We humans were made to live in community by a God who is Himself a community – three in one. On a social level, it's more joyous to view a gorgeous sunset when you can share it with someone, or to laugh at a funny story with someone who enjoys the same kind of humor than it is to do so by yourself. On a personal level, the celebrations of life are more fun when shared with those who care about you. The pain of life is a little lighter when the burden is shared with others.

God knew what He was doing when He created the blessing of friendship. Scripture reinforces that a person who has friends is experiencing a blessing from God. Celebrate your friends. Tell them how much they mean to you. Laugh together, cry together and pray together as you thank God for one another!

A friend loves at all times, and a brother is born for adversity.

Proverbs 17:17

Wounds from a friend can be trusted, but an enemy multiplies kisses.

Proverbs 27:6

Carry each other's burdens, and in this way you will fulfill the law of Christ.

Galatians 6:2

We should love one another.

1 John 3:11

Dear friends, since God so loved us, we also ought to love one another.

1 John 4:11

Do not forget to do good and to share with others, for with such sacrifices God is pleased.

Hebrews 13:16

Submit to one another out of reverence for Christ.

Ephesians 5:21

Live a life of love, just as Christ loved us and gave Himself up for us as a fragrant offering and sacrifice to God.

Ephesians 5:2

*To be able to find joy in another's joy
is the secret to happiness.*
~ *George Bernanos*

*Dear Father, what a great idea friendship
was! Thank You for my friends. We share
each other's pain and celebrate each other's
joy. Life is certainly more enjoyable because I
share it with my friends.*

Amen.

The Joy of Memories

Saying goodbye to someone you love is a heart-wrenching, painful experience – whatever the reason for the goodbye. The process of grieving the loss of a friend or loved one is a journey. A journey that can take you through anger, hopelessness, confusion and pain. Believe it or not, all those emotions are part of the healing process. Once the healing begins, memories can start to bring comfort and joy.

Memories return the joy of the former relationship – memories of laughter; memories of quiet conversations; memories of love. Don't be afraid of the pain of memories. Let the memories help take you through the pain to the pleasant joy of a relationship that was shared and appreciated.

Thank God for memory and the joy it brings. It is because of memory that those you have loved are never truly forgotten.

I thank my God every time I remember you.

Philippians 1:3

Where, O death, is your victory? Where, O death, is your sting? The sting of death is sin, and the power of sin is the law. But thanks be to God! He gives us the victory through our Lord Jesus Christ.

1 Corinthians 15:55-57

Create in me a pure heart, O God, and renew a steadfast spirit within me.

Psalm 51:10

The ransomed of the LORD will return. They will enter Zion with singing; everlasting joy will crown their heads. Gladness and joy will overtake them, and sorrow and sighing will flee away.

Isaiah 35:10

I know that my Redeemer lives, and that in the end He will stand upon the earth.

Job 19:25

I thank my God through Jesus Christ for all of you, because your faith is being reported all over the world.

Romans 1:8

I have not stopped giving thanks for you, remembering you in my prayers.

Ephesians 1:16

You will keep in perfect peace him whose mind is steadfast, because he trusts in You.

Isaiah 26:3

He lives doubly who also
enjoys the past.

~*Marcus Martial*

❧

Dear Father, my life is fuller and richer because of the memories I have. Those past experiences and relationships have helped to make me who I am today. Thank You for the joy of memories – even when they hurt at first. I'm so glad I have the memories of those I've loved, places I've been to, and things I've learned about You.

Amen.

Joy in Serving God

Are you the type of person who considers serving God to be an obligation or a joy? If you view it as an obligation, then whatever your service is; whether it's in a local church, para-church organization, or as a friend to those in need around you; whatever it is will soon feel like a chore instead of a privilege. You will find no joy at all in what you're doing.

However, if you view the opportunity of serving God as a privilege; a chance to partner with God in His work on earth; you will be filled with joy. The experience of being exactly where God wants you to be, doing the work He wants you to do is completely fulfilling.

God is working on earth, in remote places as well as in metropolitan areas. God is working and you can be a joyful participant in what He is doing!

Now, O Israel, what does the Lord your God ask of you but to fear the Lord your God, to walk in all His ways, to love Him, to serve the Lord your God with all your heart and with all your soul.

Deuteronomy 10:12

Be very careful to keep the commandment and the law that Moses the servant of the Lord gave you: to love the Lord your God, to walk in all His ways, to obey His commands, to hold fast to Him and to serve Him with all your heart and all your soul.

Joshua 22:5

"No one can serve two masters. Either he will hate the one and love the other, or he will be devoted to the one and despise the other. You cannot serve both God and Money."

Matthew 6:24

Serve wholeheartedly, as if you were serving the Lord, not men, because you know that the Lord will reward everyone for whatever good he does, whether he is slave or free.

Ephesians 6:7-8

Never be lacking in zeal, but keep your spiritual fervor, serving the Lord.

Romans 12:11

We are God's fellow workers; you are God's field, God's building.

1 Corinthians 3:9

Do your best to present yourself to God as one approved, a workman who does not need to be ashamed and who correctly handles the word of truth.

2 Timothy 2:15

Whatever you do, work at it with all your heart, as working for the Lord, not for men.

Colossians 3:23

When God calls you to do something,
He enables you to do it.

~ Robert Schuller

❧

Dear Father, what an incredible privilege it is to be able to serve You. I am constantly amazed that You allow plain, old, simple me to partner with You in Your work in this world. Thank You for giving me work to do and for equipping me to do it.

Amen.

Where's your "God-point"? What part of God's creation simply takes your breath away and causes your mental and emotional energy to focus on Him? For some people it's a snowcapped mountain set against a brilliant blue sky. For others it is the power and constancy of the ocean's tide slapping against the shore, or millions of points of bright stars in a black velvet sky. Perhaps it's when you see the gracefulness of a swan, the speed of a big cat, the massiveness of a whale ... whatever it may be, some part of nature probably directs your thoughts to God.

Stop and think about nature and God's immense creativity. He created a tiny delicate butterfly along with the splendor of a giant waterfall. He created many things for us to enjoy. Don't take His creation for granted. Celebrate it and celebrate Him as you enjoy His creativity in complete and total joy!

In the beginning God created the heavens and the earth.

Genesis 1:1

The Mighty One, God, the LORD, speaks and summons the earth from the rising of the sun to the place where it sets.

Psalm 50:1

The earth is the LORD's, and everything in it, the world, and all who live in it.

Psalm 24:1

The heavens declare the glory of God; the skies proclaim the work of His hands.

Psalm 19:1

"With My great power and outstretched arm I made the earth and its people and the animals that are on it, and I give it to anyone I please."

Jeremiah 27:5

Praise Him, you highest heavens and you waters above the skies.

Psalm 148:4

For since the creation of the world God's invisible qualities – His eternal power and divine nature – have been clearly seen, being understood from what has been made, so that men are without excuse.

Romans 1:20

Let all the earth fear the Lord; let all the people of the world revere Him. For He spoke, and it came to be.

Psalm 33:8-9

Those who contemplate the beauty of the earth find reserves of strength that will endure as long as life lasts.

~ *Rachel Carson*

❧

Dear Father, how amazingly creative You are. When I look around at this earth and see its beauty and diversity, I'm awed by what You thought of. Thank You for creating this amazing planet and for making so many things for us to enjoy and so many ways in which we can see You.

Amen.

Joy in Rest

Hard work is ... hard. It is also gratifying. A job accomplished is satisfying. For many people their self-worth is realized through their accomplishments. Others find gratification from serving others with all their energy. Some people love to get in and get dirty as they work with all their might. However, there is a necessary flip side to hard work and that is rest.

Rest allows the body, mind and spirit to rejuvenate. It's refreshing and restoring. If you're one of those people who have difficulty allowing themselves to take time to rest, remember that even God rested on the seventh day.

Find joy in a time of rest when your muscles, your mind and your heart can "catch up" and "power up" for whatever work is ahead. Appreciate the rest and let it do its work of restoration in you.

By the seventh day God had finished the work He had been doing; so on the seventh day He rested from all His work.

Genesis 2:2

May Your unfailing love rest upon us, O LORD, even as we put our hope in You.

Psalm 33:22

"Come to Me, all you who are weary and burdened, and I will give you rest."

Matthew 11:28

"Take My yoke upon you and learn from Me, for I am gentle and humble in heart, and you will find rest for your souls."

Matthew 11:29

Restore to me the joy of Your salvation and grant me a willing spirit, to sustain me.

Psalm 51:12

Restore us, O God; make Your face shine upon us, that we may be saved.

Psalm 80:3

The God of all grace, who called you to His eternal glory in Christ, after you have suffered a little while, will Himself restore you and make you strong, firm and steadfast.

1 Peter 5:10

Grace and peace be yours in abundance through the knowledge of God and of Jesus our Lord.

2 Peter 1:2

The least of things with a meaning is worth more in life than the greatest of things without it.

~ Anonymous

❧

Dear Father, rest is hard to come by because I get so caught up in the things of life. Help me, Father, to rest and in that rest to appreciate all You are and all You do for me daily. Help me, Father, to rest and listen for the sound of Your voice in the silence of that rest.

Amen.

God, in His great wisdom and kindness, has given humankind an incredible gift. Well, more than one gift, of course, but let's talk about this one – the Bible.

God communicates with you through His living Word, which teaches you how to live for Him and shares examples of saints who struggled and worked through life while learning to obey Him. The Holy Spirit can sometimes cause words to jump from the page to answer your questions or comfort your heart.

God's Word, hidden away in your heart, provides strength and encouragement no matter what trials or temptations you face.

The provision of the Bible is almost the equivalent of sitting down face to face with the Creator and having a heart-to-heart conversation. Take joy in God's Word as you read its teachings, learn from its examples and find comfort in its heart – the heart of God.

In fact, though by this time you ought to be teachers, you need someone to teach you the elementary truths of God's word all over again. You need milk, not solid food!

Hebrews 5:12

If anyone obeys His word, God's love is truly made complete in him.

1 John 2:5

All Scripture is God-breathed and is useful for teaching, rebuking, correcting and training in righteousness, so that the man of God may be thoroughly equipped for every good work.

2 Timothy 3:16-17

When Your words came, I ate them; they were my joy and my heart's delight, for I bear Your name, O LORD God Almighty.

Jeremiah 15:16

"Then you will know the truth, and the truth will set you free."

John 8:32

Your word is a lamp to my feet and a light for my path.

Psalm 119:105

These commandments that I give you today are to be upon your hearts. Impress them on your children. Talk about them when you sit at home and when you walk along the road, when you lie down and when you get up. Tie them as symbols on your hands and bind them on your foreheads. Write them on the doorframes of your houses and on your gates.

Deuteronomy 6:6-9

The precepts of the Lord are right, giving joy to the heart. The commands of the Lord are radiant, giving light to the eyes.

Psalm 19:8

If a man's Bible is coming apart,
it is an indication that he himself is
fairly well put together.

~ James Jennings

❧

Dear Father, I know I don't spend nearly enough time reading Your Word. It should be my very lifeblood. Father, give me a passion to know Your Word and let it permeate my life. Thank You for giving us Your Word and for helping and teaching us through it.

Amen.

Joy in Helping Others

There is a real joy in being able to help someone – especially someone who really needs it. It's fulfilling to meet someone's need and to let them see God's love shining through you. When you experience joy in helping others, then you're willing to go out of your way to be that helper. A benefit to being a helper is that you shift your focus off yourself and whatever problems or issues you are facing and think about others instead. This tends to make your own problems seem smaller or at least seems to put them into perspective.

Jesus is a fantastic example of Someone who helped others. Many, many times Scripture says that multitudes of people came to Him for healing and He healed them all.

When Jesus walked on this earth, He truly cared about the needs of the people around Him and He found joy in meeting their needs, even when He must have been exhausted. He is our example to serve and help whenever we see a need.

If anyone has material possessions and sees his brother in need but has no pity on him, how can the love of God be in him?

I John 3:17

Learn to do right! Seek justice, encourage the oppressed. Defend the cause of the fatherless, plead the case of the widow.

Isaiah 1:17

Two are better than one, because they have a good return for their work: If one falls down, his friend can help him up. But pity the man who falls and has no one to help him up.

Ecclesiastes 4:9-10

Each one should use whatever gift he has received to serve others, faithfully administering God's grace in its various forms. If anyone speaks, he should do it as one speaking the very words of God. If anyone serves, he should do it with the strength God provides, so that in all things God may be praised through Jesus Christ. To Him be the glory and the power for ever and ever.

I Peter 4:10-11

Therefore, as God's chosen people, holy and dearly loved, clothe yourselves with compassion, kindness, humility, gentleness and patience. Bear with each other and forgive whatever grievances you may have against one another. Forgive as the Lord forgave you.

Colossians 3:12-13

Religion that God our Father accepts as pure and faultless is this: to look after orphans and widows in their distress and to keep oneself from being polluted by the world.

James 1:27

If one part suffers, every part suffers with it; if one part is honored, every part rejoices with it.

1 Corinthians 12:26

Finally, all of you, live in harmony with one another; be sympathetic, love as brothers, be compassionate and humble.

1 Peter 3:8

Seek joy in what you give,
not in what you get.

~ Anonymous

✍

Dear Father, it means so much to be needed. Thank You for friends and loved ones who need me and whose lives I can share in. Thank You for those who share in my life. Their help means so much – I know I'm never alone because You are with me, but I'm also so grateful for those people who help me through life day by day.

Amen.

Joy Because of Forgiveness

"Dear God, let me be the person my puppy thinks I am." You know how forgiving a puppy is, right? You can scold him, leave him alone for hours on end, forget to walk him ... and he still greets you with unrestrained enthusiasm.

How many times do you think, "Wow, I blew it today!"? Do you wonder how many times your family, friends, and even God, can forgive you? Guess what? Everybody feels that way once in a while, even if they don't admit it.

The joy to be thankful for today is that of forgiveness. Our families and friends forgive our shortcomings and failures and keep right on loving us, just as we do for them. And God, well, His forgiveness just goes on and on. His unrestrained love for you is the reason He forgives. God is love, so no matter what, God must love. In order to love His imperfect children, He must forgive us.

"This is My blood of the covenant, which is poured out for many for the forgiveness of sins."

Matthew 26:28

In Him we have redemption through His blood, the forgiveness of sins, in accordance with the riches of God's grace.

Ephesians 1:7

For the sake of Your name, O LORD, forgive my iniquity, though it is great.

Psalm 25:11

"I will cleanse them from all the sin they have committed against Me and will forgive all their sins of rebellion against Me."

Jeremiah 33:8

"Forgive us our debts, as we also have forgiven our debtors."

Matthew 6:12

"If you forgive men when they sin against you, your heavenly Father will also forgive you."

Matthew 6:14

If we confess our sins, He is faithful and just and will forgive us our sins and purify us from all unrighteousness.

I John 1:9

"Do not judge, and you will not be judged. Do not condemn, and you will not be condemned. Forgive, and you will be forgiven."

Luke 6:37

We need not climb into heaven to see whether our sins are forgiven; let us look into our hearts, and see if we can forgive others. If we can, we need not doubt that God has forgiven us.

~ *Thomas Watson*

❧

Dear Father, I'm so eager to accept forgiveness but often I'm not very willing to offer it. Thank You for generously forgiving me. Thank You when those around me forgive me. Please Father, give me the strength and grace to forgive others when I need to – following Your example.

Amen.

Joy in the Midst of Trials

We are all familiar with the Scripture verse, "Consider it pure joy, my brothers, whenever you face trials of many kinds" (James 1:2) Let's stop there for a moment. Do you read that verse and think, "Really? Are you serious, God? Do you want me to jump up and down and cheer when life gets really stinky?" Yeah, that's what it sounds like. Now, let's look at the second part of this verse, "because you know that the testing of your faith develops perseverance. Perseverance must finish its work so that you may be mature and complete, not lacking anything."

So trials can have a purpose. This is not to say that God brings trials into your life, sometimes life just happens.

But your response to trials: leaning on God, seeking His guidance, trying to react and respond in a way that brings honor to Him, learning through the trial, is a perseverance that makes your faith stronger and develops your spirit to be more Godlike. That's a reason for joy!

We also rejoice in our sufferings, because we know that suffering produces perseverance; perseverance, character; and character, hope.

Romans 5:3-4

May the Lord direct your hearts into God's love and Christ's perseverance.

2 Thessalonians 3:5

Therefore, since we are surrounded by such a great cloud of witnesses, let us throw off everything that hinders and the sin that so easily entangles, and let us run with perseverance the race marked out for us.

Hebrews 12:1

Consider it pure joy, my brothers, whenever you face trials of many kinds, because you know that the testing of your faith develops perseverance.

James 1:2-3

Perseverance must finish its work so that you may be mature and complete, not lacking anything.

James 1:4

In this you greatly rejoice, though now for a little while you may have had to suffer grief in all kinds of trials. These have come so that your faith – of greater worth than gold, which perishes even though refined by fire – may be proved genuine and may result in praise, glory and honor when Jesus Christ is revealed.

1 Peter 1:6-7

Just as the sufferings of Christ flow over into our lives, so also through Christ our comfort over-flows.

2 Corinthians 1:5

He has not despised or disdained the suffering of the afflicted one; He has not hidden His face from him but has listened to his cry for help.

Psalm 22:24

We could never learn to be brave
and patient if there were only joy
in the world.

~ Helen Keller

❧

Dear Father, it's really hard to be thankful for trials. I'm glad they make me grow stronger in my faith, but to be honest ... they aren't fun. Father, help me to be strong, to look for the lessons You want me to learn, and to lean on You. Help me to learn to be thankful for what trials bring into my life.

Amen.

Joy in Discovering Gifts

God has called His children to do special work for Him. The Scriptures also state that each person's work is important to God's kingdom and His work on this earth. God gives each of His children the gifts and abilities needed to do the job He has called them to do.

But how do you know what those gifts are? The process of discovery is exciting. Start with determining what you like to do; what brings you great pleasure. Next, listen to the people around you ... what do they say you are good at? What things do you do that people commend you on? Put those two things together. More than likely that's the area that God has gifted you in. Look around you and see how your passion and your gifts can be put together to serve God and the people around you.

What joy there is in discovering how God has gifted you and how you can use those gifts to serve Him!

And now, O Israel, what does the Lord your God ask of you but to fear the Lord your God, to walk in all His ways, to love Him, to serve the Lord your God with all your heart and with all your soul, and to observe the Lord's commands and decrees that I am giving you today for your own good?

Deuteronomy 10:12-13

Be very careful to keep the commandment and the law that Moses the servant of the Lord gave you: to love the Lord your God, to walk in all His ways, to obey His commands, to hold fast to Him and to serve Him with all your heart and all your soul.

Joshua 22:5

Now fear the Lord and serve Him with all faithfulness.

Joshua 24:14

Serve wholeheartedly, as if you were serving the Lord, not men, because you know that the Lord will reward everyone for whatever good he does, whether he is slave or free.

Ephesians 6:7-8

Never be lacking in zeal, but keep your spiritual fervor, serving the Lord.

Romans 12:11

For we are God's fellow workers; you are God's field, God's building.

1 Corinthians 3:9

Do your best to present yourself to God as one approved, a workman who does not need to be ashamed and who correctly handles the word of truth.

2 Timothy 2:15

Whatever you do, work at it with all your heart, as working for the Lord, not for men, since you know that you will receive an inheritance from the Lord as a reward. It is the Lord Christ you are serving.

Colossians 3:23-24

*Thanks be to God, who made us
His captives and leads us along
in Christ's triumphal procession.
Now wherever we go He uses us
to tell others about the Lord
and to spread the Good News
like a sweet perfume.*
~ *The Apostle Paul (2 Cor. 2:14 NLT)*

Dear Father, sometimes I feel like I've got nothing special to offer You – no real way to serve You. Thank You for the reminder that You have a way for me to serve You that is uniquely molded for me. Thank You for gifting me to do the job You have for me.

Amen.

Joy in Christ's Resurrection

Imagine how Jesus' followers must have felt as His dead body was dragged down from the cross and carried to the cave to be buried. Can you sense their hopelessness and confusion? It must have seemed as if everything they thought was going to happen – all the plans they had – died on the cross with Jesus.

Of course, we have the benefit of looking at that experience from a rearview mirror. We know that God's plan didn't end with Jesus' death, but instead actually picked up speed because of it. That, of course, is because Jesus defeated death and came back to life. His resurrection carried God's plan forward.

Praise God for His plan to bring you and all His children into a personal relationship with Himself.

Praise God for the promise of eternity with Him and of victory over death for all who choose to know God!

Jesus said to her, "I am the resurrection and the life. He who believes in Me will live, even though he dies."

John 11:25

I want to know Christ and the power of His resurrection and the fellowship of sharing in His sufferings, becoming like Him in His death.

Philippians 3:10

Praise be to the God and Father of our Lord Jesus Christ! In His great mercy He has given us new birth into a living hope through the resurrection of Jesus Christ from the dead.

1 Peter 1:3

For you know that it was not with perishable things such as silver or gold that you were redeemed from the empty way of life handed down to you from your forefathers, but with the precious blood of Christ, a lamb without blemish or defect.

1 Peter 1:18-19

"The Son of Man did not come to be served, but to serve, and to give His life as a ransom for many."

Matthew 20:28

God demonstrates His own love for us in this: While we were still sinners, Christ died for us.

Romans 5:8

Who is he that condemns? Christ Jesus, who died – more than that, who was raised to life – is at the right hand of God and is also interceding for us.

Romans 8:34

What I received I passed on to you as of first importance: that Christ died for our sins according to the Scriptures, that He was buried, that He was raised on the third day according to the Scriptures.

I Corinthians 15:3-4

Jesus Christ is God's everything for man's total need.

~ Richard Halvorsen

Dear Father, thank You for Christ's victory over death. Your plan would not have been complete if Jesus had stayed in the grave. Thank You for Your power, Your love and the promise of eternal life with You!

Amen.

Joy Because of Family

Family members are the people who know you best. They know your good points and your bad ones. You can't fool family members with fancy words or bluffs because they know the real you. After all, they live with you. Most people are more completely themselves when they are at home than anywhere else.

Family members may make you crazy and frustrate you terribly, but when push comes to shove, you would do anything in the world for them and they would do the same for you. You may get angry at them, but you would never let anyone else say negative things about them! Family members love you no matter what and the memories you share with them are priceless. Having a family is a real gift from God. Family is precious because you are connected at the heart and you belong, for better or worse. There's a sense of security in that.

Ruth replied, "Don't urge me to leave you or to turn back from you. Where you go I will go, and where you stay I will stay. Your people will be my people and your God my God."

Ruth 1:16

How good and pleasant it is when brothers live together in unity!

Psalm 133:1

Be devoted to one another in brotherly love. Honor one another above yourselves.

Romans 12:10

But if serving the LORD seems undesirable to you, then choose for yourselves this day whom you will serve, whether the gods your forefathers served beyond the River, or the gods of the Amorites, in whose land you are living. But as for me and my household, we will serve the LORD.

Joshua 24:15

Sons are a heritage from the LORD, children a reward from Him.

Psalm 127:3

Train a child in the way he should go, and when he is old he will not turn from it.

Proverbs 22:6

In the presence of the LORD your God, you and your families shall eat and shall rejoice in everything you have put your hand to, because the LORD your God has blessed you.

Deuteronomy 12:7

Finally, all of you, live in harmony with one another; be sympathetic, love as brothers, be compassionate and humble.

1 Peter 3:8

A happy family is but
an earlier heaven.
                              ~ John Bowring

❧

Dear Father, sometimes my family makes me crazy. But the honest, truthful, bottom line is that I love them dearly. Thank You so much for each one of them. Thank You for their love, support, laughter and care. Thank You that I can share in their lives, too. Draw us closer and closer, Father.

                              Amen.

Joy in Laughter

How great is it to have a good, deep belly laugh? The kind where tears run down your cheeks? Life can be pretty serious so the opportunity to laugh so hard that you can barely catch your breath is one to appreciate. Do you know that it's good for you to laugh like crazy? Laughter is energizing and freeing, and even has health benefits as it gets the endorphins flowing.

Laughter is a gift from God. He knew how much we would need it sometimes and how much it would help our attitudes and emotions.

Another wonderful thing about laughter is the joy of sharing it with someone. When you've really laughed with someone, you've shared an important experience that you'll later recall with joy and fondness. Laughter builds bridges and makes people feel at home. Look for joyful opportunities to laugh.

Our mouths were filled with laughter, our tongues with songs of joy. Then it was said among the nations, "The LORD has done great things for them."

Psalm 126:2

A cheerful heart is good medicine, but a crushed spirit dries up the bones.

Proverbs 17:22

Let all who take refuge in You be glad; let them ever sing for joy. Spread Your protection over them, that those who love Your name may rejoice in You.

Psalm 5:11

You have made known to me the path of life; You will fill me with joy in Your presence, with eternal pleasures at Your right hand.

Psalm 16:11

The LORD is my strength and my shield; my heart trusts in Him, and I am helped. My heart leaps for joy and I will give thanks to Him in song.

Psalm 28:7

I will rejoice in the LORD, I will be joyful in God my Savior.

Habakkuk 3:18

You have made known to me the paths of life; You will fill me with joy in Your presence.

Acts 2:28

He will yet fill your mouth with laughter and your lips with shouts of joy.

Job 8:21

Shared laughter creates a bond of friendship. When people laugh together, they cease to be young and old, master and pupils, worker and driver. They have become a single group of human beings, enjoying their existence.

~ W. Grant Lee

❧

Dear Father, I simply cannot imagine life without laughter. It eases the stresses and pains. It draws me closer to those with whom I laugh. Thank You, Father, for the gift of laughter. May I enjoy it often!

Amen.

Joy ... in the Long Run

You've heard the expression, "Can't see the forest for the trees." Life is really like that sometimes, isn't it? The details of day-to-day life and the problems that pop up in it can be overwhelming. Those details and accompanying problems can steal your joy very quickly. Of course, once you begin focusing on those problems, every day begins with a dark cloud hanging over it.

So what do you do? Take an emotional step back. Stop looking at the trees and focus on the forest for a while. Ask God to help you see how the struggles you are dealing with right now fit into a bigger picture. Remember that God is in control of the big *and* the small stuff.

As you see a bigger view of life, you can celebrate the joy that lies ahead ... in the long run.

"Submit to God and be at peace with Him; in this way prosperity will come to you."

Job 22:21

I will lie down and sleep in peace, for You alone, O LORD, make me dwell in safety.

Psalm 4:8

You will keep in perfect peace him whose mind is steadfast, because he trusts in You.

Isaiah 26:3

The fruit of the Spirit is love, joy, peace, patience, kindness, goodness, faithfulness, gentleness and self-control. Against such things there is no law.

Galatians 5:22-23

Let the peace of Christ rule in your hearts, since as members of one body you were called to peace. And be thankful.

Colossians 3:15

May God Himself, the God of peace, sanctify you through and through. May your whole spirit, soul and body be kept blameless at the coming of our Lord Jesus Christ.

I Thessalonians 5:23

Flee the evil desires of youth, and pursue righteousness, faith, love and peace, along with those who call on the Lord out of a pure heart.

2 Timothy 2:22

"Be still, and know that I am God; I will be exalted among the nations, I will be exalted in the earth."

Psalm 46:10

*Man is fond of counting his troubles
but he does not count his joys.
If he counted them up as he ought to,
he would see that every lot has enough
happiness provided for it.*

~ Fyodor Dostoevsky

❧

Dear Father, thank You first of all for Your patience with me. When I get stuck looking at the trees and can't see the forest, thank You for guiding my vision. Thank You that in the long run – even through pain and discouragement – I can experience joy because of Your love.

Amen.

Joy Because of God's Help

Help. When you really need it, help is so very welcome. Knowing that someone cares about you enough to go out of his or her way to help you is such a comfort. The experience of helping each other builds community as people partner together and understand that others care about them. Receiving and appreciating help makes you more willing to help others.

The most amazing help comes from God Himself. Just think about it, the Creator of the universe, who surely has very important things to do – like handling wars, disease and natural calamities – actually cares about *you* and the problems you face.

He cares about the things that occupy your mind, the things that tie your stomach in knots or cause anxiety in your heart. He cares. In fact, He not only cares, He even acts on your behalf. God will help you with whatever you face, just ask Him.

Blessed are you, O Israel! Who is like you, a people saved by the LORD? He is your shield and helper and your glorious sword. Your enemies will cower before you, and you will trample down their high places.

Deuteronomy 33:29

But You, O God, do see trouble and grief; You consider it to take it in hand. The victim commits himself to You; You are the helper of the fatherless.

Psalm 10:14

In my distress I called to the LORD; I cried to my God for help. From His temple He heard my voice; my cry came before Him, into His ears.

Psalm 18:6

The LORD is my strength and my shield; my heart trusts in Him, and I am helped. My heart leaps for joy and I will give thanks to Him in song.

Psalm 28:7

Because He Himself suffered when He was tempted, He is able to help those who are being tempted.

Hebrews 2:18

So we say with confidence, "The Lord is my helper; I will not be afraid. What can man do to me?"

Hebrews 13:6

Trust in the LORD with all your heart and lean not on your own understanding; in all your ways acknowledge Him, and He will make your paths straight.

Proverbs 3:5-6

"Do not let your hearts be troubled. Trust in God; trust also in Me."

John 14:1

Do not pray for easy lives. Pray to be stronger men. Do not pray for tasks equal to your powers. Pray for powers equal to your tasks.

~ Phillips Brooks

Dear Father, so many times I try to live life in my own strength ... and fail. I'm so thankful for Your help and strength that gets me through life. Father, thank You for helping me, even when I forget to ask. Thank You for strengthening me, even when I'm not aware of it. Thank You for always paying attention to me and knowing what I need.

Amen.

Joy Because of Prayer

What an incredible privilege mankind has to be able to communicate with God. He arranged the miracle of prayer Himself. Isn't it amazing that God actually wants His people to talk with Him? He does – He wants to know what's on your heart. He cares about what worries you and what causes you to celebrate. He cares enough to want to know. The Scriptures encourage you to talk with Him. They reinforce that God wants to hear from you and loves the opportunity to communicate with you.

The Old Testament heroes had the benefit of hearing God's voice – direct communication from Him. You have the same privilege today – you may communicate with God about whatever is on your heart. But when you hear His voice, you must be still and listen. He will communicate with you.

The God of Creation, the God of everything, wants to have a conversation with you. He loves you. Amazing, isn't it?

"If My people, who are called by My name, will humble themselves and pray and seek My face and turn from their wicked ways, then will I hear from heaven and will forgive their sin and will heal their land."

2 Chronicles 7:14

The LORD has heard my cry for mercy; the LORD accepts my prayer.

Psalm 6:9

The LORD is far from the wicked but He hears the prayer of the righteous.

Proverbs 15:29

"But I tell you: Love your enemies and pray for those who persecute you."

Matthew 5:44

"When you pray, go into your room, close the door and pray to your Father, who is unseen. Then your Father, who sees what is done in secret, will reward you."

Matthew 6:6

Very early in the morning, while it was still dark, Jesus got up, left the house and went off to a solitary place, where He prayed.

Mark 1:35

Be joyful in hope, patient in affliction, faithful in prayer.

Romans 12:12

Pray continually.

1 Thessalonians 5:17

Prayer is exhaling the spirit of man and inhaling the spirit of God!
~ *Edwin Keith*

❧

Dear Father, I'm so sorry that the privilege of prayer is one I sometimes take for granted. When I stop and think about it, I'm amazed that You want to talk with me. You want to hear how I'm doing, what is concerning me or what I'm celebrating. Thank You so much for the joy of talking with You every day!

Amen.

Joy Because of the Hope
of Eternity

Eternity is a long time. Forever. Can you imagine living forever with the struggles and problems of this life? Not too appealing, is it? Well, thankfully, the Christian's eternity is profoundly more hopeful than that. God promises you eternity with Him; in heaven where there is no pain, no sorrow – just the opportunity of praising Him forever.

No one really knows what heaven will be like. But one speculation is that the joy of eternity with God will mean doing the things you love and enjoy the most – using the gifts and talents He gave you – throughout eternity to praise and worship Him. That's an amazing thought, isn't it? Imagine doing what you love to do forever in praise and worship to God.

When you accept God's promise of forgiveness of sin, appreciate and receive the sacrifice of Jesus, and trust in the hope of eternity with Him, you can celebrate life with joy!

"Oh, that their hearts would be inclined to fear Me and keep all My commands always, so that it might go well with them and their children forever!"

Deuteronomy 5:29

I saw the Holy City, the new Jerusalem, coming down out of heaven from God, prepared as a bride beautifully dressed for her husband.

Revelation 21:2

"In My Father's house are many rooms; if it were not so, I would have told you. I am going there to prepare a place for you. And if I go and prepare a place for you, I will come back and take you to be with Me that you also may be where I am."

John 14:2-3

However, as it is written: "No eye has seen, no ear has heard, no mind has conceived what God has prepared for those who love Him."

I Corinthians 2:9

"Blessed are the poor in spirit, for theirs is the kingdom of heaven."

Matthew 5:3

"Store up for yourselves treasures in heaven, where moth and rust do not destroy, and where thieves do not break in and steal."

Matthew 6:20

Our citizenship is in heaven. And we eagerly await a Savior from there, the Lord Jesus Christ, who, by the power that enables Him to bring everything under His control, will transform our lowly bodies so that they will be like His glorious body.

Philippians 3:20-21

I press on toward the goal to win the prize for which God has called me heavenward in Christ Jesus.

Philippians 3:14

The surest mark of a Christian is not faith, or even love, but joy.

~ *Samuel Shoemaker*

✍

Dear Father, how could I not be filled with joy when I think of the promise of eternity with You. Forever! Thank You for Your plan that made possible the hope of sharing Your heaven and being with You forever.

Amen.

Joy in Loving Others

Love is a characteristic of God. The Bible says God is Love, so in reverse it must be true that Love is God. Therefore, when you show love to those around you, you are actually showing them what God is like.

Do you take joy in an opportunity to show love to those around you? Now loving your friends and family is easy, right? After all, you care about them and want to do what you can to make their lives better.

Does the joy of loving others extend to those who are not your closest friends or loved ones? Are you willing to get out of your comfort zone to show love to others?

How special it is to be God's hands to someone, to speak His words of kindness, to show love to someone who really needs it. Take joy in the privilege of loving others.

"Do not seek revenge or bear a grudge against one of your people, but love your neighbor as yourself. I am the LORD."

Leviticus 19:18

Know therefore that the LORD your God is God; He is the faithful God, keeping His covenant of love to a thousand generations of those who love Him and keep His commands.

Deuteronomy 7:9

So be very careful to love the LORD your God.

Joshua 23:11

If I speak in the tongues of men and of angels, but have not love, I am only a resounding gong or a clanging cymbal.

1 Corinthians 13:1

"A new command I give you: Love one another. As I have loved you, so you must love one another. By this all men will know that you are My disciples, if you love one another."

John 13:34-35

"My command is this: Love each other as I have loved you."

John 15:12

Who shall separate us from the love of Christ? Shall trouble or hardship or persecution or famine or nakedness or danger or sword?

Romans 8:35

Love does no harm to its neighbor. Therefore love is the fulfillment of the law.

Romans 13:10

If God is thy Father,
man is thy brother.
~ Alphonse de Lamartine

❧

Dear Father, I know that You are joyous when we love one another and share in one another's lives. That is how we show one another who You are. Thank You, Father, that You didn't create us to live in solitude, but to live in community with one another. Thank You for the people in my life.

Amen.

Joy in the Midst of Sadness

When you are sad and someone continually tries to cheer you up, how do you react? Yeah, it's frustrating. Sometimes you just need to be sad and that's okay.

But there are also times when you need to be honest and admit that you're enjoying wallowing in your sadness. What will help you find joy in your life again? There are a few things – remember that you're never alone because God promised to be with you always. Remember that the dark days you're experiencing now will not last forever.

The reality that God loves you and cares about every detail of life that upsets you or worries you is the reason you can still have joy in the midst of sadness. He cares about what you're going through and if you lean on Him and seek His guidance, in His time, He will walk you out of your problems.

I have been crucified with Christ and I no longer live, but Christ lives in me. The life I live in the body, I live by faith in the Son of God, who loved me and gave Himself for me.

Galatians 2:20

Because of His great love for us, God, who is rich in mercy, made us alive with Christ even when we were dead in transgressions – it is by grace you have been saved.

Ephesians 2:4-5

How great is the love the Father has lavished on us, that we should be called children of God! And that is what we are! The reason the world does not know us is that it did not know Him.

1 John 3:1

This is how we know what love is: Jesus Christ laid down His life for us. And we ought to lay down our lives for our brothers.

1 John 3:16

The LORD is good, a refuge in times of trouble. He cares for those who trust in Him.

Nahum 1:7

Cast all your anxiety on Him because He cares for you.

1 Peter 5:7

Those who know Your name will trust in You, for You, LORD, have never forsaken those who seek You.

Psalm 9:10

The LORD is my strength and my shield; my heart trusts in Him, and I am helped. My heart leaps for joy and I will give thanks to Him in song.

Psalm 28:7

As gold is purified in the furnace,
so the faithful heart
is purified by sorrow.
~ *Giovanni Guarini*

Dear Father, it is a good reminder that joy and sorrow are inseparable. Thank You that no matter what pain comes, I can know with certainty that things will get better. Thank You that whatever sorrow I go through, I know that I'm never alone because You've promised to be right there with me.

Amen.

Joy in Work

Do you enjoy working? Do you take pleasure in a job well done when you've invested the effort of hard work mentally, physically and emotionally? Hopefully, you do find joy in work. God has placed you in the position you hold at the place where you work.

It may be that your eight-to-five job is not something you are passionate about. That's okay. God may have you there because of the influence you can have on your co-workers. If you are fortunate enough to work at a job where God has uniquely gifted you, thank Him daily and shine with joy in the work you do.

God has chosen to partner with people to accomplish His purposes on earth. The ability to work, both at a money-earning job and in volunteer work, is a blessing. Thank God for the ability, strength and opportunity to work.

The Lord God took the man and put him in the Garden of Eden to work it and take care of it.

Genesis 2:15

Be strong and courageous, and do the work. Do not be afraid or discouraged, for the Lord God, my God, is with you. He will not fail you or forsake you until all the work for the service of the temple of the Lord is finished.

I Chronicles 28:20

The Lord will fulfill His purpose for me; Your love, O Lord, endures forever – do not abandon the works of Your hands.

Psalm 138:8

All hard work brings a profit, but mere talk leads only to poverty.

Proverbs 14:23

The sluggard's craving will be the death of him, because his hands refuse to work.

Proverbs 21:25

She sets about her work vigorously; her arms are strong for her tasks.

Proverbs 31:17

"Do not work for food that spoils, but for food that endures to eternal life, which the Son of Man will give you. On Him God the Father has placed His seal of approval."

John 6:27

You yourselves know how you ought to follow our example. We were not idle when we were with you, nor did we eat anyone's food without paying for it. On the contrary, we worked night and day, laboring and toiling so that we would not be a burden to any of you. We did this, not because we do not have the right to such help, but in order to make ourselves a model for you to follow.

2 Thessalonians 3:7-9

The secret of joy in work is contained in one word – excellence. To know to do something well is to enjoy it.

~ *Pearl S. Buck*

༄

Dear Father, I have to admit that sometimes I get really tired of working. But at the same time I admit that I enjoy the satisfaction of a job well done. Thank You for the strength and opportunity to work. Help me to always do my best with whatever task is set before me.

Amen.

Joy Because of Second Chances

You've blown it ... in a relationship ... at work ... with God. Is the relationship gone forever? Hopefully not. Is the job gone? Hopefully not. Will God turn His back on you? Never. When you've made mistakes, hurt a friend or loved one, or disappointed God, a second chance is what you hope for. You want the opportunity to make things right and when those second chances come, aren't you incredibly grateful?

When second chances come in human situations, you can be sure God's hand has been directing forgiveness and love. When the second chance comes from God Himself, there are several opportunities to learn. There is the opportunity to learn from your mistake or disobedience, which means there is the opportunity for growth.

There is also the opportunity to realize, once again, how very much God loves you. He wants you to grow and learn because He loves you. Celebrate second chances.

Let all who take refuge in You be glad; let them ever sing for joy. Spread Your protection over them, that those who love Your name may rejoice in You.

Psalm 5:11

Turn, O Lord, and deliver me; save me because of Your unfailing love.

Psalm 6:4

Your love is ever before me, and I walk continually in Your truth.

Psalm 26:3

You are forgiving and good, O Lord, abounding in love to all who call to You.

Psalm 86:5

Because of His great love for us, God, who is rich in mercy, made us alive with Christ even when we were dead in transgressions – it is by grace you have been saved. And God raised us up with Christ and seated us with Him in the heavenly realms in Christ Jesus.

Ephesians 2:4-6

It is by grace you have been saved, through faith –
and this not from yourselves, it is the gift of God.

Ephesians 2:8

All the prophets testify about Him that everyone
who believes in Him receives forgiveness of sins
through His name.

Acts 10:43

In Him we have redemption through His blood,
the forgiveness of sins, in accordance with the
riches of God's grace.

Ephesians 1:7

Profound joy of the heart is like a magnet that indicates the path of life. One has to follow it, even though one enters into a way full of difficulties.

~ *Mother Teresa*

❧

Dear Father, all the cares of failure after failure are forgotten in the joys of one more chance. Thank You for never giving up on me and for giving me opportunity after opportunity to learn, grow and obey.

Amen.

Joy Because of Scripture's Stories

The Bible is God's Word. It's His message of love to you. It is also His instruction for how He desires you to relate to the world around you, as well as to Him. It offers guidance for decisions and choices. The Bible also contains the stories of God's history with mankind. As you read through the life stories of Moses, Noah, David, Esther, Ruth, Peter, Paul and others, you see their weaknesses as well as their victories.

The stories of Scripture show the humanity of God's followers. By allowing their mistakes to be recorded, God shows us His forgiveness and His tenacity in holding on to His children. Their stories show you how to pick yourself up, confess your failures and shortcomings, accept God's forgiveness and then move forward.

The stories in Scripture are lessons wrapped in encouragement. Take joy in reading those stories and learning from them!

He who conceals his sins does not prosper, but whoever confesses and renounces them finds mercy.

Proverbs 28:13

If you confess with your mouth, "Jesus is Lord," and believe in your heart that God raised Him from the dead, you will be saved.

Romans 10:9

For the sake of Your name, O LORD, forgive my iniquity, though it is great.

Psalm 25:11

"I will cleanse them from all the sin they have committed against Me and will forgive all their sins of rebellion against Me."

Jeremiah 33:8

Everything that was written in the past was written to teach us, so that through endurance and the encouragement of the Scriptures we might have hope.

Romans 15:4

All Scripture is God-breathed and is useful for teaching, rebuking, correcting and training in righteousness.

2 Timothy 3:16

Moses was faithful as a servant in all God's house, testifying to what would be said in the future.

Hebrews 3:5

We do not want you to become lazy, but to imitate those who through faith and patience inherit what has been promised.

Hebrews 6:12

The Bible dramatically deals with difficulties that discourage us, temptations that test us, and problems that plague us. It richly reveals the Christ who can change us, the Friend who can free us, and the Light who can lead us.

~ William A. Ward

❧

Dear Father, I'm so thankful for the stories in Scripture. Thank You for sharing the struggles, setbacks and moments of failed faith of the heroes of Scripture. Thank You for wrapping those stories with faith, love and trust. Thank You for showing me that the Christian life is a journey.

Amen.

Joy Because of God's Love

When you stop and think about it, doesn't it simply amaze you that the God of all things; the God who created the universe ... loves you? Really, think about all the incredibly BIG things He has to watch over.

Think about the major prayers people are sending to Him about really important things ... things you might feel are more world-effecting and more important than your simple little requests. Yet, He not only takes the time for you, but He *wants* to hear from you.

He longs for a relationship with you. God instructs over and over in Scripture that you should talk to Him, listen for His response, read His Word so you get to know Him. Why does He say these things? Not because He's on some power trip but because, quite simply, He loves you. He loves you.

I am like an olive tree flourishing in the house of God; I trust in God's unfailing love for ever and ever.

Psalm 52:8

May the Lord direct your hearts into God's love and Christ's perseverance.

2 Thessalonians 3:5

Keep yourselves in God's love as you wait for the mercy of our Lord Jesus Christ to bring you to eternal life.

Jude 21

Give thanks to the LORD, for He is good; His love endures forever.

I Chronicles 16:34

I trust in Your unfailing love; my heart rejoices in Your salvation.

Psalm 13:5

How priceless is Your unfailing love! Both high and low among men find refuge in the shadow of Your wings.

Psalm 36:7

When I said, "My foot is slipping," Your love, O Lord, supported me.

Psalm 94:18

How great is the love the Father has lavished on us, that we should be called children of God! And that is what we are!

1 John 3:1

*You don't have to be afraid of
praising God too much;
unlike humans He never
gets a big head.*

~ Paul Dibble

*Dear Father, praising You for Your love and
care is the greatest joy of my life. Thank You
for Your constant unconditional love. Thank
You for Your patience when I fail to love You
back. Teach me to love You more and more.*

Amen.

Joy in Disappointment

It's easy to be filled with joy and a celebratory attitude when things are going well. When you're healthy, your family is all getting along and work is good, joy comes pretty easily. However, when things in life start falling apart, you probably turn to God, asking for His intervention and help. How do you feel when God seems to be silent? Can you still find joy while working through the disappointment of unanswered prayer?

God asks you to pray and He promises to hear your prayers. So how do you handle it when He seems to be silent? Remember who God is. His character is that He is Love, so He cannot not love. It would go against His character to do so. So even in the disappointment that comes from God's silence, remember that He still loves you. That never changes.

Know that He must have a better plan ahead for you. Wait on Him and be filled with joy in the meantime.

In the morning, O LORD, You hear my voice; in the morning I lay my requests before You and wait in expectation.

Psalm 5:3

Wait for the LORD; be strong and take heart and wait for the LORD.

Psalm 27:14

My soul waits for the Lord more than watchmen wait for the morning, more than watchmen wait for the morning.

Psalm 130:6

The LORD longs to be gracious to you; He rises to show you compassion. For the LORD is a God of justice. Blessed are all who wait for Him!

Isaiah 30:18

Christ was sacrificed once to take away the sins of many people; and He will appear a second time, not to bear sin, but to bring salvation to those who are waiting for Him.

Hebrews 9:28

Be patient, then, brothers, until the Lord's coming. See how the farmer waits for the land to yield its valuable crop and how patient he is for the autumn and spring rains.

James 5:7

Even though I walk through the valley of the shadow of death, I will fear no evil, for You are with me; Your rod and Your staff, they comfort me.

Psalm 23:4

May Your unfailing love be my comfort, according to Your promise to Your servant.

Psalm 119:76

Something can be learned from the smallest as well as the greatest disappointments or frustrations. A child who drops his ice-cream cone and is not given the money for another will learn to be more careful next time. A man whose car runs out of fuel will learn to check his tank more closely in the future.

~ Christine Lindeman

❧

Dear Father, the lessons learned from disappointment are painful lessons. It must be hard for You, too, to see Your children in pain. Thank You, though, for caring enough to teach us those lessons and thank You that You walk with us through the pain of disappointment.

Amen.

Joy in Peace

Wow, peace in this crazy, busy world is a real gift, isn't it? Being at peace is like an emotional oasis in the midst of chaos.

Everything in life fights against peace and Satan slides right into that pattern by encouraging you to keep your life so busy that you have no time for peace.

That busyness even fights against your time with God, infringing on that commitment so there is no quiet time to hear His gentle voice of guidance. Pretty soon you feel like you're running on a hamster wheel and peaceful moments are only a distant memory.

This is not the way God wants your life to be, my friend. He knows that you need the rejuvenation of peace in your life. Peaceful times allow for the quietness from which God can speak. Peaceful times give rest to your soul. Seek peace. Seek to have quiet times that allow your mind, spirit and body to rest.

Consider the blameless, observe the upright; there is a future for the man of peace.

Psalm 37:37

A heart at peace gives life to the body, but envy rots the bones.

Proverbs 14:30

For to us a child is born, to us a son is given, and the government will be on His shoulders. And He will be called Wonderful Counselor, Mighty God, Everlasting Father, Prince of Peace.

Isaiah 9:6

You will keep in perfect peace him whose mind is steadfast, because he trusts in You.

Isaiah 26:3

"I have told you these things, so that in Me you may have peace. In this world you will have trouble. But take heart! I have overcome the world."

John 16:33

The mind of sinful man is death, but the mind controlled by the Spirit is life and peace.

Romans 8:6

Whatever you have learned or received or heard from me, or seen in me – put it into practice. And the God of peace will be with you.

Philippians 4:9

Let the peace of Christ rule in your hearts, since as members of one body you were called to peace. And be thankful.

Colossians 3:15

*Peace is the deliberate adjustment of
my life to the will of God.*

~ *Anonymous*

Dear Father, that quote is so telling. Any time
I struggle against Your will, I will have no
peace. I thank You, Father, that perfect peace
is found in obeying You. Help me, Father, to
do that more and more.

Amen.

Joy in Being Loved

Is there anything more confidence-building, ego-boosting, smile-inducing in the world than knowing you are loved? Absolutely knowing that there is someone, whether it be a family member, friend or significant other, who unconditionally loves you; someone who helps you believe in yourself to the point where you are just a bit more willing to reach for the stars.

When someone loves and believes in you, don't you want to live up to their faith in you? Yes, that love helps you become a better person. Stop right now and think about the people in your world. Whose love are you completely confident in? Do they have that same confidence in your love for them? Tell them how much you appreciate their love and support in your life and offer that same unconditional love back to them.

Then, bow your head and thank God for the gift of love and those people in your life who bring you such joy!

Surely goodness and love will follow me all the days of my life, and I will dwell in the house of the LORD forever.

Psalm 23:6

The eyes of the LORD are on those who fear Him, on those whose hope is in His unfailing love.

Psalm 33:18

Great is Your love, higher than the heavens; Your faithfulness reaches to the skies.

Psalm 108:4

"My command is this: Love each other as I have loved you."

John 15:12

"Greater love has no one than this, that he lay down his life for his friends."

John 15:13

Let no debt remain outstanding, except the continuing debt to love one another, for he who loves his fellowman has fulfilled the law.

Romans 13:8

Over all these virtues put on love, which binds them all together in perfect unity.

Colossians 3:14

May the Lord make your love increase and overflow for each other and for everyone else, just as ours does for you.

1 Thessalonians 3:12

We need to be loved and we need to give love. When we are thwarted in this, we suffer terribly.

~ G. H. Montgomery

❧

Dear Father, when everything seems to be going wrong and I begin to lose faith in myself, it is the love of those around me that often pulls me back to a centered place. Thank You for placing people in my life who love me and by their love remind me of Your constant love, Lord.

Amen.

Joy Because There Is a Plan

Are you a planner? Do you have a notebook filled with lists and notes for every event you are a part of? Do you like to have your life planned out or do you enjoy "free-floating"? Sometimes spontaneity is fun, but in the important things of life, isn't it nice to know that there is a plan? It's nice to know that someone is in control.

Well, praise God, He is in control. He has a plan, in fact, He has had one since the beginning of time. How amazing to think that even before you took your first breath in this life, God had a plan for you. He had already created the plan of how you could come to know Him through the birth, life, death and resurrection of Jesus. He already knew what gifts and talents you would have.

What a peaceful, joyful thought it is that God has a plan for you – just for you.

I trust in You, O LORD; I say, "You are my God."

Psalm 31:14

When I am afraid, I will trust in You.

Psalm 56:3

Trust in Him at all times, O people; pour out your hearts to Him, for God is our refuge.

Psalm 62:8

Trust in the LORD with all your heart and lean not on your own understanding; in all your ways acknowledge Him, and He will make your paths straight.

Proverbs 3:5-6

"For I know the plans I have for you," declares the Lord, "plans to prosper you and not to harm you, plans to give you hope and a future."

Jeremiah 29:11

The kingdom of God is not a matter of eating and drinking, but of righteousness, peace and joy in the Holy Spirit.

Romans 14:17

Let the peace of Christ rule in your hearts, since as members of one body you were called to peace. And be thankful.

Colossians 3:15

Grace and peace to you from Him who is, and who was, and who is to come, and from the seven spirits before His throne, and from Jesus Christ, who is the faithful witness, the firstborn from the dead, and the ruler of the kings of the earth.

Revelation 1:4-5

Joy is perfect acquiescence in God's will because the soul delights in God Himself.

~ H. W. Webb-Peploe

❧

Dear Father, how grateful I am that You have a plan – not just the grand, incredible plan for salvation – though that is amazing in itself. But also that You have a detailed plan for my life. I'm so glad to know that things don't just happen by chance or due to circumstance. You know what You're doing and You know what I'm doing. Thank You for Your plan.

Amen.

Joy Because of God Himself

The Creator. Our Protector. Our Friend. Our Advocate. The Lamb of God. The Resurrection and Life. The Good Shepherd. The Cornerstone. The Bread of Life. The Savior. The Master Teacher. The Living Water. The Alpha and Omega. The True Vine. The Light of the World. Everlasting Father. Prince of Peace. Immanuel. Jehovah Jireh. Jehovah Shalom. Jehovah Sabaoth. El Shaddai. Adonai.

These are just some of the many names of God. Each name reflects a different aspect of His character and the way He relates to us. Which characteristic of God calls out to you the most? Which one fills your heart with joy and warmth?

What an amazing God He is, He meets you just where you are – where your need is greatest. He fills that need ... and more. Thankfully and completely, He is God and He is Love.

The LORD your God has blessed you in all the work of your hands. He has watched over your journey through this vast desert. These forty years the LORD your God has been with you, and you have not lacked anything.

Deuteronomy 2:7

I will be glad and rejoice in You; I will sing praise to Your name, O Most High.

Psalm 9:2

The LORD lives! Praise be to my Rock! Exalted be God my Savior!

Psalm 18:46

Many, O LORD my God, are the wonders You have done. The things You planned for us no one can recount to You; were I to speak and tell of them, they would be too many to declare.

Psalm 40:5

Then Jesus declared, "I am the bread of life. He who comes to Me will never go hungry, and he who believes in Me will never be thirsty."

John 6:35

"Whoever believes in Me, as the Scripture has said, streams of living water will flow from within him."

John 7:38

"I am the good shepherd; I know My sheep and My sheep know Me – just as the Father knows Me and I know the Father – and I lay down My life for the sheep."

John 10:14-15

For in Scripture it says: "See, I lay a stone in Zion, a chosen and precious cornerstone, and the one who trusts in Him will never be put to shame."

1 Peter 2:6

There are souls in this world who have the gift of finding joy everywhere and of leaving it behind them wherever they go.

~ *Frederick W. Faber*

❧

Dear Father, all You are is amazing. Thank You for meeting each one of us exactly where we are and providing in our needs and caring for our hearts. When I think of all You are to me, joy is my only response.

Amen.